THE
ULTIMATE
MARKETING
ASSET

THE ULTIMATE MARKETING ASSET

The Ultimate Marketing Weapon That Will Cut Your Lead Generation Costs in Half, Increase Your Ad Budget From $0, and Bring You A Steady Stream of Clients Willing To Pay For Your Authority, Credibility, and Expertise!

JEROME LEWIS
ALICE BRIGGS

The Ultimate Lead Marketing Asset

ISBN: 978-1-948666-43-5

Published by:
Alice Arlene Ltd Co Press
Lubbock, TX

Dedicated to all those who go on the adventure of real estate entre-prenurship, may all you do succeed.

Contents

Part 1: The Lead Generation Magnet 1

Part 2: How to Write a Book 5

    Introduction. 7

    My Story 9

    The Power of a Book 11

    Choose Your Most Important Points 13

    Writing the Book 17

    Beta Readers. 21

    Final Touches. 23

    If and Where to Publish. 25

    Time Frames 27

Part 3: Indie Route 101 31

    Quick Start Map 33

    Why Indie? 37

    KU vs Wide 43

Text vs Image 51

Research 55

Editing 59

Formatting 63

Cover Design 67

Meta Data 81

Publish 85

Marketing 89

Resources 91

Author Note 93

Part 4: Real Estate Deal Acquisition Secrets 97

Foreword 99

Introduction 101

Deal Acquisition Frustration Elimination 103

Why Should You Listen To Me? 105

Closed Deals Come From Leads 107

Lead Generation Is Only 1 Part of Your Business 109

Math Matters & Success Is In The Percentages 111

The Fortune Is In The Followup 113

Social Media Yields Fast and Efficient Results 115

So What Do I Do Next? 117

Other Resources 121

About The Author 125

Work With Us 127

THE
ULTIMATE
MARKETING
ASSET

PART 1

The Lead
Generation Magnet

MY NAME IS Jerome Lewis and let me tell a quick story about how I discovered the Ultimate Lead Generation Magnet. I used to work in retail as a cashier earning a minimum wage of $7.25/hour. I used to work at a supermarket, and I was so frustrated with that job that I wanted to change something. I went online. I did some "Googling" and discovered that the best way to get wealthy is through real estate. It's said, that most millionaires become so through real estate.after learning this new information, I began to explore and research real estate investing. One of my most burning questions, once I got into the business, was: "How can I get people to sell their houses to me as a real estate investor or.... to utilize my services as a real estate agent?" As hard-working real estate entrepreneurs, it feels extremely exhausting to be *used* for all your hard work, time, talent, and energy... Only for that seller/lead/prospect/client to go with another real estate professional's services. This is what is happening most of the time with real estate professionals.

Understanding those frustrations myself, I wanted to find a solution to minimize that problem or get rid of it completely.

Internally, I wanted more leads for my business so I could work toward my personal, professional, and financial success. I began by researching ways to generate leads for my business only to discover that:

- paid services wanted too much money,
- couldn't guarantee results
- barely understood marketing and lead generation

I then decided to go all-in on learning marketing. I learned major principles, strategies, and tactics from legends such as Ron LeGrand, Dan Kennedy, Darcy Juarez, Russell Brunson, Krista Mashore, GoGo Bethke, Kevin Donlin, Davin Fesmire, Aaron Foster, and *many many more.*

One thing I learned particularly was the importance and effectiveness of paid marketing and paid advertising. Paid strategies can literally change your life fast! When done correctly and strategically, using paid strategies can yield you results immediately and predictably.

Everything I learned, I was excited to share with my colleagues, students, and business partners.

Putting together the many things I learned from great mentors and coaches, I was able to come up with what I like to call the Ultimate Lead Generation Magnet or The Ultimate Marketing Asset. These items are part of a larger system that my company has developed and we call that, The Ultimate Real Estate Marketing Implementation System.

These are strategies and tactics that we use in our business and use with our clients and students to help them come up with effective marketing campaigns. My ultimate objective as a real estate entrepreneur myself was to give back to my peers.

This book is the start of that journey and I welcome you to be part of this journey with me — starting with this book. My teaching and delivery style is to include as much practical information as possible. However, I do also understand that some people appreciate details and personal stories. If you want the full and more details story, please refer to your included companion guide at https://UltimateMarketingAsset. com/Free-Gift.

In this book, I was privileged to collaborate with Alice Briggs and we're going to help you understand the importance of developing The Ultimate Lead Generation Magnet for your business. If you're a serious entrepreneur, you will appreciate what you learn because it will help you become the expert and authority to your clients, prospects, and customers.

This book is actually 3 in 1. Jump in where ever you need the information, or start at the beginning.

- In Part 2, Alice will show you how quick and easy it can be to create this lead generation magnet.
- In part 3, Alice will show you how to take your manuscript and get it into a book.
- In part 4, I'll be back to show you how to use this incredibly powerful tool to maximize your business.

Let's get started!

PART 2

How to Write a Book

Alice Briggs

Introduction

AS A NOT as busy as you would like yet experienced real estate entrepreneur, you know that one of the biggest difficulties in building your business is getting new clients in your door. You can (and I'm sure you do) ask your clients to refer their family and friends, but while they mean well, this is often problematic.

Some reasons for this breakdown in communicating the benefits of your treatment may include:

1. Your client may not clearly understand all the benefits you provide.
2. Your client may not describe your business in a way that is appealing to someone unfamiliar with your industry.
3. Your client may not understand all of the people and situations you are an expert in, they only know how you've helped them.
4. Your client may have a difficult time expressing the broad scope of what you do. Their perspective is too narrow.

A surprising solution to most of these issues is to publish a small book about the benefits you provide for your clients. You then give out copies to your current clients who can then pass them on to others. It's much easier than you may think, and just because it's a book, the perceived importance and value that your potential client places on the information inside may significantly increase their desire and follow through to make that initial appointment.

Before you become overwhelmed, I'm not talking about a four-hundred-page tome. No, in this case, shorter is better. Far better. It's easier for you to create, and your client is much more likely to give it to their friends and family, and more likely that those people will read it. And by short, I mean one hundred pages or fewer.

You can easily take client testimonials, before and after illustrations, and client stories that show all the benefits you can provide. Give two copies to each client, and ask them to share with others they know who could benefit from what you do. You'll be amazed at how many more new clients we'll be calling you. Some have documented an increase from a 10% to 60% referral rate.

The key is that it's a book.

A book has a high perceived value. People believe books are difficult to write and produce, so they are impressed when they hold your book in their hand. And people are more likely to read and act on what's inside.

In this book, I'm not only going to tell you how you can create such a book for your patients, but I'm going to show to you the truth of how easy it is just because I wrote this book for you. The principle is the same. The perceived importance of the format lends weight and believability to my words.

CHAPTER 1

My Story

WHEN I FIRST started my inner healing practice, I created helpful worksheets for my clients so they could maximize their progress while they worked with me. I had them beautifully designed in full color. I compiled them into folders that I gave to my clients on their first visit. They smiled and politely thanked me.

A year or two later, I learned how to independently publish. I took those worksheets, expanded them a bit, and created a short book. It's been available on Amazon ever since. When I ran out of worksheets, I ordered copies of the book instead to give to my clients.

What happened then astounded me.

Not only were my clients much more visibly impressed that I was giving them a book at the end of that first session, but they brought the books back. They read them. They used them. I saw flags and highlights throughout the book when they asked for clarification on a point or two in their next session.

And—most importantly—they also made much faster progress toward their goals in working with me than they had previously.

The only difference was the information was in book form.

My clients valued the format of the information more, so they were more willing to apply the information and increase their transformation. Just because I put it in a book.

CHAPTER 2

The Power of a Book

THROUGHOUT HISTORY, BOOKS have held status and importance. Even if you're not a reader, there's something inspiring about visiting an extensive library, especially one with old books. To walk through the halls of ancient texts is to walk the paths of the influential thinkers of history.

And while the modern age has given us vast quantities of information with a few keystrokes, the printed word still impresses and delights us.

The perception of writing a book is that it takes years and tons of research. It's a significant undertaking and not one to be entered into lightly. And there is a place for those kinds of books.

But that's not what I'm recommending for you here.

You don't have time for that.

And it won't actually do as much good as it could.

No, I recommend you borrow on the perceived value of a book but streamline the process so that the book takes weeks, not years.

Imagine in two or three months when you're handing out a book that you've written to your clients, and they pass them on to their friends and family.

And then your phone starts ringing.

It's very doable, and I will show you how in the pages that follow.

In fact, I'm doing exactly what I'm telling you to do. I've written about thirty books and am a well-practiced writer, so I may be faster than you, but I am tracking my time in this process to show you how quickly you can go from idea to book in hand.

And by the way, if you have no interest in writing or don't have time to do so, my team and I can do everything I'm going to talk about for you. You can schedule a call with us here if you're convinced that you want to have your treatment protocols created as books but don't want to do the work yourself.

CHAPTER 3

Choose Your Most Important Points

I DON'T DO EXACTLY what you do, so I'm going to make a few assumptions as a fairly logical person.

You probably have different information that you give to different people based on their needs or wants, right? I imagine there are some similarities, and the basic information of how you work, your philosophy of business, etc., will be the same. But there might be enough differences that you can see the value of having more than one referral book.

But don't start there unless you have a team in place to do this for you.

What is the most common problem people come to you to solve? Start there. If you want to keep a list going of the others, that's perfectly fine, but don't try to do more than one at a time. It will slow you down and frustrate you.

By choosing the one you see the most in your business, you will see the biggest return on your investment of time, effort, and money while you're learning the process.

List the Elements

Gather the information you already have and determine what information you need to make the book as complete as possible.

1. Do you have information—printed, on video, or otherwise—that you already use to explain how you can help people?
2. What should prospective clients know about how you can help them? Write a list of those. Just jot down brief bullet points.
3. What information do you have in place?
4. Is there anything else you need to create or gather?
5. Over the next little while, pay attention to your interactions with clients, is there anything missing in the above?
6. Are there any patient testimonials or stories that would help illustrate how you help people?
7. Is there anything else that you could add or create that would help to clarify or illustrate the benefits? E.g., before and after images, illustrations, charts, etc.

You don't have to violate client confidentiality, if that applies, to include testimonials and stories. General stories are fine, and they help the information resonate with your clients in a deeper way. Show them the success they can have if they work with you.

Organize It

When you have all the information gathered, list everything in the order that makes the most sense, and will be the most helpful for prospective clients to know.

You don't have to write the book in order, but you will need to organize the points for your clients before you complete it.

If you put the points in a logical order, then others can more easily assist you in completing your book as well. Maybe you have staff to help you with this, and you do not personally do this. If so, enlist them in this process as quickly as possible.

Outline

Once you have put the information in order, then it's time to outline your book. You don't have to get very detailed here. Remember that we don't want to get bogged down with creating the book. We just want you to be able to work as efficiently as possible. You're busy, and there's no need for this process to take any more time than necessary.

My typical outline is the chapter title and then three or four bullet points of what I want to cover in that chapter. For this book, I created a list of the elements I wanted to write about and gathered those points into chapters that I thought would be the easiest for you to follow. This isn't cast in concrete, so don't get too bogged down here, but if you have an outline to follow, you can more easily write sections or chapters here and there throughout your day or week.

Keep your outline with you. The format doesn't matter. Some people love technology and do everything digitally; others still prefer pencil and paper. Some find 3x5 cards helpful. There is no right or wrong way to write a book. Just find the method that works best for you. If you have your outline with you, you can quickly dictate a section or chapter while you're waiting in line or in traffic or commuting to and from work. Keep track of what you've completed so you aren't duplicating your work.

You want to set yourself up for success so that you can continue to move forward with your book. Your biggest problem will be getting distracted or overwhelmed and quitting. Above all, I don't want that for you.

CHAPTER 4

Writing the Book

Writing

I'll talk more about the mechanics of writing shortly, but let me reiterate here that there is no right or wrong way to write a book. The point is to get it done; the how depends on you and what works best for you and your schedule.

Do you work better with a sizeable chunk of time set aside? If so, then can you check yourself into a hotel for a day or two and write the book?

Or will it work better for you to set aside thirty minutes a day or every few days to work on short sections at a time?

And don't say, "What good will thirty minutes do?"

You know how powerful thirty minutes are. What would happen if your clients spent thirty minutes three times a week following your plan?

We overestimate what we can do in larger blocks of time, but underestimate what we can do in small bits of time. Consistency is the key. If you can devote one hour a week or thirty minutes three times per week, you will be amazed at how quickly you can finish your book. Obviously, the more frequently you block out time to write, the faster you will finish. So if you write for thirty minutes six times a week, then you'll finish twice as fast.

But be realistic about how much time you have or where you can carve it out during the writing process. And give yourself grace in this process if things go wrong. Don't let one missed day keep you from going back the next. You can do this.

Dictation

When people talk about writing a book, they often think of someone sitting at a typewriter or picking up a pen and paper. Those aren't very common in reality because they are slow. Although, again, if that's what works for you, then go for it.

I'm currently working in a word processing program on my laptop. Any word processor will work for a book of this size. You don't need a special program.

You're not limited to actual writing though. Dictation is an excellent alternative and one that may work very well for you, especially if you are used to using dictation in your practice.

You want the tone of your book to be casual and friendly. Talk to your prospective patient, not at them. Often, dictation will help you achieve that conversational style because you are speaking, not writing. We often communicate in more formal language when we write, and dictating can bypass that formality.

Dictation can also be much faster, which is not an insignificant consideration for your busy life and business.

If you have a smart phone, then you can use the voice recorder on your phone to dictate sections of your book. Start each recording with the chapter title and section or topic so that you can easily organize and arrange the content later.

For instance, I would say, "Chapter 4: Dictation," and then dictate what I wanted to say in this section. Keep track of what you've dictated so you can organize the transcriptions when you get them.

Transcription

If you dictate, then you'll need to have the audio transcribed into text. You may have a service that you currently use that would be willing and able to do this for you.

Numerous apps, some paid and some free, also transcribe with some measure of success. You may wish to test several to find one that works best for you. Rev, Otter, and Descript are excellent options at the time of this writing, but the artificial intelligence behind such services is evolving rapidly, so better options may be available by the time you're reading this and ready to get started.

You're looking for a program that can fairly accurately interpret your words and get them into printed form. Most will send you a text file, or you can copy/paste the words into your word processing program.

I recommend placing these into your document in the order of your outline so you can keep track of which sections you've completed and which ones you still need to do.

Review

You'll need to review the transcriptions or hire someone to do this for you. We all use filler words and the transcriptions do not always accurately reflect what you've said. Keep your audio files as well so you can refer back to them to clarify the content if needed.

At this point, I should probably emphasize that you don't have to do this yourself. You can hire someone to compile the transcriptions and all the other elements of your book. This is part of the service that my team provides, but freelancers are available as well. No matter who does this, someone will need to review the transcriptions and compare them with the audio to ensure their accuracy.

Illustrations, Charts, Images, and More

As you are writing your book, consider if illustrations, charts, images, or any other such visual information would help clarify your benefit for your prospective patient.

Do you have before and after images and stories? Include them. Other people's stories are highly motivating and encouraging.

You do need to be aware of who owns the copyright to any illustrations, charts, images, or other visual information you've gathered over the years. Images need to be appropriately sourced or created. You can purchase stock images from various sites, but check the licensing to make sure that they are available for your use and for resale in a book.

You will avoid any copyright infringement issues if you create your own resources, so this is what I recommend. This does add complexity to the creation of your book, but copyright infringement fees can be very steep, so it's a great investment in your peace of mind.

CHAPTER 5

Beta Readers

ONCE YOU'VE COMPILED all the information in your book, it's great practice to have beta readers review the material. These are people similar to your clients—regular people who aren't familiar with the contents of the book.

Their job is to read the book and see if it makes sense. We all have blind spots, and wording that we think is clear may be very confusing to others. Beta readers are people similar to your target audience who read your book and let you know if they find any holes, gaps, or points of confusion.

I recommend that you choose a handful of people. You don't want too many because that adds complexity you don't want or need. But you do want more than one or two so that if all agree that a certain area is confusing, you'll know it needs to be addressed.

Give these people a PDF or document version of your book and ask them to read it. Ask them for specific feedback, such as

- Does the book makes sense?
- Do they feel they understood it well?
- Do they feel they understand how you could help them?

- Do they understand the illustrations, images, or charts?
- Is there anything that they don't understand?
- Did they get lost at any point?

I recommend including a form they can fill out and take notes on as they go through your book.

When you get the information back, make the necessary changes. You do not have to accept every suggestion that the beta readers give you. But if four of them tell you that the fifth point is confusing, then you should probably listen to their advice.

CHAPTER 6

Final Touches

Editing

I do not recommend trying to skimp on editing. I'm a pretty strong writer, but my editor still makes numerous changes that make my message clearer.

There are different levels of editing, depending on how much work your book needs. I cover all of those in more detail in *Indie Route 101*, which in included later in this book.

So I'll just reiterate here that you do need an editor and that most editors will take a look at a sample of your book, give you a sample edit, and then provide you with a quote for the cost.

Editing is typically priced on a per-word fee, so your short treatment protocol will not be as expensive to have edited as a large four-hundred-page treatise.

When your book comes back from the editor, review their edits. A competent editor will not change your voice. Your book should still sound like you, just more polished. But you will want to make sure they haven't inadvertently changed the meaning of anything you've said. Most are happy to discuss their changes and help you maintain your meaning while ensuring grammatical accuracy.

Formatting

Once your book has been edited, you can have it formatted. This is the process of taking your manuscript and making it look like the inside of a book.

Again, I go over all the details in *Indie Route 101*, but your main considerations will be
- Trim size: What size will your book be? Common sizes for short books are 5x8 or 6x9 if you have a lot of worksheets.
- Where will you print?

Also consider the average age of your clients. If they are boomers or older, you may wish to produce a large print edition so that anyone with visual issues can easily access your book.

Cover Design

Once the inside has been prepared for printing, you'll also need a cover for your book. You'll need a front cover, back cover, and spine—we call that the full-wrap. The spine width is determined by the number of pages as well as the color and quality of the paper.

I recommend you seek professional help for both formatting and cover design. For a busy professional, the time and effort it takes to learn to do these tasks is not a strong return on your investment. To be fair, my team provides these services, so I am biased, but I also know what it took in time, software, education, and practice to learn to do these tasks well. Properly prepared files increase the perceived value of your book and will save time in printing as the files will be correct.

You can hire freelancers or use a full-service team like I have for a one-stop shop.

CHAPTER 7

If and Where to Publish

F OR YOUR PURPOSE of creating an effective patient referral book, you don't have to technically publish the book. You can have the book printed by a local or national printer and just order copies as you need them.

But you can easily publish your book on Amazon or on many other platforms if you so choose. *Indie Route 101* can walk you through that process.

If you decide to publish, then you'll want to purchase an ISBN, and you may choose to register the copyright for your book. An ISBN is an international identification number that tells all the various points in the publishing industry that a book with this number is yours. You purchase them from Bowker in the US.

Whenever you create something, you own the copyright by default at the time of creation. You can register a copyright with the government if you so choose. This allows for more legal protection should you need to take someone to court for copyright infringement. Neither of these is required even if you publish your book.

However, if your book is specific to your business and your clients, then you might not benefit by actually publishing.

A local printer may provide you with the best printing quality for the most reasonable price, and you'll save on shipping charges as well. If you don't have a local printer, I can recommend Ingram Spark. They are a nationwide printer with an excellent reputation. I use them. You can order books as you need them from a few to a few hundred or a few thousand. They allow you to use a SKU instead of an ISBN if you choose not to publish and distribute your book.

CHAPTER 8

Time Frames

'VE NOW SPENT five hours writing this book of about forty-five hundred words.

Short is good.

Let's crunch some numbers based on my experience writing this book, which is similar to what I'm suggesting that you do. I know this subject well and talk about it often, so don't have to concentrate as I write out this information. I'm just getting what is in my head out into the world where it can benefit you and others.

And that's all I'm suggesting and recommending that you do for your clients.

For the ease of math, let's say you can write or dictate five hundred words per hour. This is slower than what I've just demonstrated, but I prefer to err on the side of conservative examples and set myself up for as much success as possible when making these calculations.

If your treatment protocol is five thousand words, then you'll need about ten hours; if it's ten thousand words, you'll need twenty hours.

If you go into the office early and spend an hour writing, you'll have a five-thousand-word book written in ten days or two weeks and a ten-thousand-word book written in twenty days. If you only have thirty minutes a day, then double those figures (twenty and forty days, respectively). (Ten-thousand words or less is a good length.)

Considering the longest time of forty days at five days per week, that's eight weeks.

A reasonable estimate for the other people involved is

- Transcription: one week
- Beta readers: two weeks
- Edits: two weeks
- Formatting and cover design: two weeks
- Printing and shipping: three weeks

Note that most of the above time is not yours and those time frames may vary considerably, depending on the availability of each of these individuals. You've hired these people to work on your project while you are doing what you normally do in your daily life and business.

From start to finish, you can have a book from idea to in-hand copies ready to pass out in roughly twelve to eighteen weeks, maybe even faster depending on how quick your team is.

And this is with as little as two weeks of your time working on the writing around your other day-to-day activities.

That's doable, isn't it?

Indie Route 101

Alice Briggs

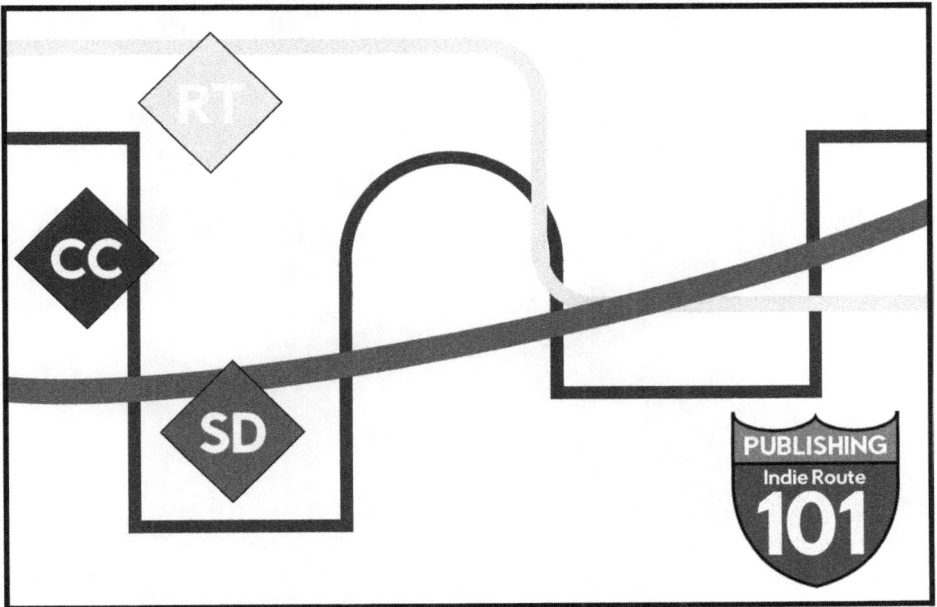

CHAPTER ZERO

Quick Start Map

T HOUGH BRIEF, THIS book still covers a lot of ground. I'm giving you publishing ideas, no matter where you are in your journey. Publishing has a lot of moving pieces, so you can easily bite off too much at once. The biggest reason for this is that new authors try and do everything all at once. Please don't do this!

None of the steps are extraordinarily difficult although they each require work. Many authors publish every day, so these steps are definitely doable. I recommend that you choose your desired course of action and take one step at a time until you have completed that step. Then take the next step. This will help you so that you don't become stressed out and keep you moving toward your goal of holding your finished, published book in your hand.

Feel free to read through the entire book, but please don't become overwhelmed. You can do this! Authors just like you do so every day.

Choose your publishing adventure!

The Sunday Drive: This is perfect for new authors publishing their first book. I recommend you start with Kindle Unlimited and a text-based book (see p. 52). Watch for this symbol throughout the book.

1. Choose your format: Kindle Select eBook–p. 44
2. Edit–p. 59
3. Formatting: Done for you, ePub only–p. 64
4. Premade cover design: JPG–p. 72
5. Metadata–p. 81
6. Upload to KDP for Kindle Unlimited–p. 85

The Road Trip: This is perfect for a published author who wants to expand their reach or a new author who is willing to take a few more steps before they publish their book. I recommend you add a print version of your book through KDP. You may also be a children's book author with an image-based book (see p. 21). Watch for this symbol throughout the book.

1. Choose your format: KDP Print– p. 44
2. Edit–p. 59
2. Formatting: Done for you, ePub and PDF–p. 64
3. Custom cover design: JPG and PDF–p. 73
4. Metadata–p. 81
5. Upload to KDP–p. 85

The Cross Country: This is the most complex journey. You can choose which pieces you want to do and when you want to do them. You don't have to do them all at once. Avoid overwhelm by choosing an additional piece and adding it as you're able. Watch for this symbol throughout the book.

1. Choose your formats: ebook, print, and audio–p. 44
2. Edit–p. 59
2. Formatting DIY: ePub, and PDF–p. 65
3. Custom cover design: JPG, and PDF for KDP and Ingram Spark (IS)–p. 73
4. Metadata–p. 81
5. Deselect Kindle Select if you selected it previously
6. Upload to additional providers
7. Ask Ingram Spark to transfer your title from KDP

CHAPTER ONE

Why Indie?

A S YOU ENTER the publishing realm, you'll encounter entirely new vocabulary, which can be very confusing. I'll start by defining a few terms to clarify I mean in the pages that follow.

Traditional publishing means that an agent represents you and submits your book to a publisher. If accepted, they pay you an advance and take the rights to your book. An advance is pre-payment against the royalties they expect the book to earn. So you need to earn out that advance before you receive any more money. You typically split any royalties or advances with your agent. The barrier to entry here is very high, and the time frame for publication can take from nine to twenty-four months.1

Vanity publishing is a predatory outfit that acts as your publisher at great expense to you. You pay them; they do not pay you, and they often also require you to sign over the rights to your book. They may also provide you with very expensive but poor-quality services, such as editing and cover design. You may also have to purchase large quantities of your book at exorbitant prices.

A Full service author services company will provide you with a variety of in-house services to prepare your manuscript for publication. Prices and quality of services vary. This type of publishing overlaps somewhat with vanity publishers, so buyer beware, but legitimate companies will do a good job for you and your book.

Indie or independent publishing is when you act as the general contractor for your book. You remain in full control of the process and hire people to do parts of the process that you can't or don't want to do for yourself.

Self-publishing has become nearly a meaningless term, as most of the above, except traditional publishers, will refer to themselves as self-publishers. I define self-publishing as someone who does every step themselves. Very few people can effectively handle all aspects of their publishing journey, but this can be a viable place to start. You can then hire professionals as you are able. Downsides exist for this, especially with covers and editing, but people have bootstrapped their books and then upgraded elements later when they could.

---

1   Robert Lee Brewer, "How Long Does It Take to Get a Book Published?" Writer's Digest, June 9, 2020, https://www.writersdigest.com/getting-published/how-long-does-it-take-to-get-a-book-published.

I am proudly indie, but this book won't dictate what you should do or how you should do it. The following are some factors to consider as you determined which path to choose.

Accessibility

With traditional publishing, you are at the mercy of finding an agent to read, accept, and sell your book. Not all publishers accept all genres. Publishing has traditionally been a tightly controlled industry with formidable gatekeepers.

Vanity publishers have been around for many years. They are so named because they appeal to your vanity—a published title regardless of merit in exchange for a large sum of money. Many have pivoted and call themselves self-publishers. And here is where the labels become very murky.

Some full-service companies offer an out-of-the-box publishing services and do a decent job for authors for a reasonable fee. But others charge exorbitant prices for inferior work.

Publishing is now accessible to all, and that is a fabulous opportunity, but it also creates a buyer-beware environment for those who want a quick fix.

Quality

A common misconception is that self-published books are inferior in quality to traditionally published titles. And that's a fair assessment from many, to be sure.

However, when you are fully indie, you can have your book polished to the highest standard. You can also continuously improve the quality of your work. You can fix typos and upload revised files, and there will be typos, even in traditionally published books.

You can absolutely produce a product that meets or exceeds the quality of traditionally published titles.

Speed

Unquestionably, indie publishing is a much faster process than traditional publishing. The fastest you can hope to have a traditionally published title available for purchase by your readers is around nine to twelve months. Some indie-published authors manage to publish in that many days. Granted, that's faster than most, and they may have streamlined their process over time, but it's not unheard of. You can even publish that fast to a high standard if you plan ahead and write quickly.

Agility

Agility relates to and depends on speed. But aside from initial publishing, you can also change and revise parts of your book, such as your blurb and covers as trends change or as you learn more about what your readers want. Changes for most of these things are as simple as copying and pasting new text onto your dashboards. Test and measure what is more effective if you desire.

Also, when it comes to quality, you can correct typos as you find them or a few times a year, whatever you like. And soon, your book is perfect!

Control

I've touched some on this above, but I feel that it warrants its own section. When you go indie, you are the contractor of the building that is your book. You are free to DIY or hire professionals, depending on your desires and capabilities. You are also free to decide where to publish and distribute your book, which I'll address more in the next chapter.

And if you make an error, you are free to readjust and continue on better than before.

Retention of Intellectual Property Rights

When you create something, you are the copyright owner of your creation with few exceptions, such as work for hire. Copyright, at least in the United States, lasts for seventy-five years after your death. When you publish, consider the long-term implications of what you're doing, not just for yourself, but also for your heirs for a couple of generations.

Keeping the rights of your work also means that you can do many things with it. Depending on the type of book you're producing, you can license the rights for audio, merchandise, and film. Or you can handle some of those things yourself.

Royalties

Traditionally published authors receive around 10–15 percent of the purchase price in royalties, and they may have to split that with their agents. Depending on where you publish or distribute, you can earn as much as 85 percent in royalties as an indie author.

Marketing

For me, the major benefit of being a traditionally published author would have been someone to market for me. And while that does happen for a few big-name authors, for the vast majority, a traditional publisher won't even consider someone without an existing platform or the capability to have a built-in market.

Backlist

Your backlist is all your previously published titles. Traditional publishers mostly—if not entirely—ignore this mine of potential revenue. They promote new releases, but have you ever seen an ad for a book that's been out for a couple of years? Probably not. Yet, if you've signed over your rights to your IP, then all of that work just sits. Whereas, if you still have the rights to your book, you can also encourage readers to find your backlist titles, and hopefully they will read everything you've written so far. If your profit from a book is five dollars and you only promote your most recent title, then you'll earn five dollars for each reader who finds you. But if you have a backlist of ten titles and the reader goes back and reads them all, you've now earned an additional fifty dollars from that reader.

You also can promote books in your backlist that relate to current events. Imagine if you had published a book on surviving pandemics in 2015. When March 2020 hit, you ran a few ads to that book. It probably would have sold very well.

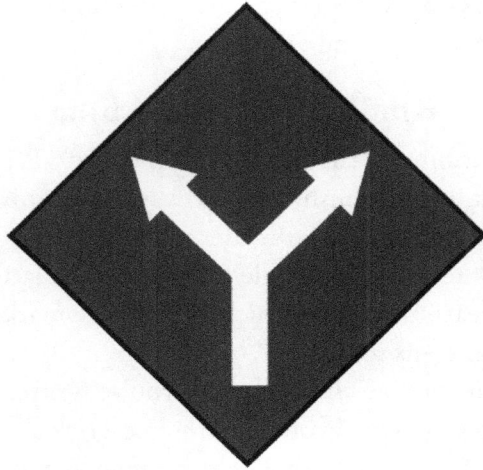

CHAPTER TWO

KU vs Wide

I NDIE AUTHORS CHOOSE one of two paths for publishing: exclusive with KDP in KU or what they call "wide," meaning world-wide through other distributors. This is for e-books, as the exclusivity requirements for KDP's Kindle Select or Kindle Unlimited apply to e-books only. Both are viable options, and authors can make a lot of money with both. Choose the one that fits with what you want and that best fits your marketing strategy.

I was in KU for the first few years of my publishing career and then went wide. I've heard of others who are wide and then go into KU, and still others have a hybrid approach, so you are not making a permanent decision. Do be aware that many readers are only KU or on other platforms, and others do both, so if you are marketing to KU readers, they may not follow you wide and vice versa.

Kindle Direct Publishing

KDP has revolutionized the publishing industry. Prior to Amazon's KDP, you could indie publish in a few ways, but Amazon provided a means to connect the potential reader with the indie author through the Kindle. This remains the single most popular platform for readers and authors, at least in the US, which is a massive market. It is also one of the easiest platforms to use.

It's important to note that although you've written one book, you have at least two products if you do both an e-book and print. The distributors treat them separately, though they are linked on your dashboard and on the product pages that the reader sees.

Ebook

Your e-book is more like a webpage than a book in function. You can upload a mobi file, which is Amazon's proprietary format, or an ePub, which other e-book retailers accept as well.

You can choose between a 35 percent and a 70 percent royalty rate, which is not as simple as it sounds. The 70 percent royalty rate comes with some restrictions. Your price must be between $2.99 and $9.99, the list price of the print book must be at least 20 percent more than the e-book, and it must be available in all geographies for which you have rights. This usually means all, unless you've sold or given those rights to someone else. They will also charge you a delivery fee, which can be significant if you have a lot of images. You will need to do the math to see which percentage makes the most economic sense for your book. Amazon has a calculator that does the math for you as you upload your book. This is my preferred method.

If you are not also in Kindle Select, you will not be eligible for the 70 percent royalty for sales in Brazil, Japan, Mexico, and India. Your royalty rate in those countries will be 35 percent. You should consider this if those are your primary markets.

There are a few requirements for books in the 35 percent royalty rate. The maximum price is $200, and the minimum depends on the size of the file delivered. Link to details in the footnotes.2

Kindle Select is the author facing name of Kindle Unlimited, the exclusive subscription available through Amazon. For a monthly fee, readers can read any title enrolled in the program for "free". KDP pays authors based on the number of pages read. They calculate payment in some mysterious way that changes and announce the new rate each month. Over the last four years, this payment has ranged from $.004 to $.0053.

If you enroll in Kindle Select, you can have a maximum of 10 percent of the material available digitally in any other form anywhere else. This does not include print or audio. You can have print and audio versions of your book available outside of Amazon, but not the ebook. You can have a short excerpt of your book on your website, for example, but typically not 2-3 chapters.

---

2   https://kdp.amazon.com/en_US/help/topic/G200634560.

Print

KDP Print is the print-on-demand arm of Amazon's indie author platform. This was formerly called Create Space, which merged with KDP Print in 2018. You now have one dashboard for both e-book and print, and the function is largely the same.

Print on demand (POD) means that KDP prints your book only if and when someone purchases it. This could be you purchasing author copies or a reader purchasing on Amazon. This differs from the traditional method of printing hundreds or thousands of copies, storing them, and shipping them to bookstores. Because of the nature of the process, POD tends to have a larger tolerance or wiggle room to allow for your design. Traditional off-set printing is more accurate, but the tradeoff is a large upfront expense and boxes of books stashed in the garage or under the bed. Some authors do sell enough on their own to do offset printings of their books, so this isn't a complete either/or choice as long as you have your own ISBN. (See Chapter 8 for more information on ISBNs.)

Paperback is the only format available through KDP Print, currently, although additional formats are rumored to be in beta at the time of this writing. Royalties for books sold on Amazon marketplaces are 60 percent less the cost to print the book. Royalties for expanded distribution are 40 percent less the cost to print the book. When you upload your book, KDP has calculators that will show you what your royalty will be in the various areas. I also recommend that you research expected prices within your genre and categories, but we'll discuss that in a later chapter.

KDP offers quite a wide range of trim sizes, the term that refers to the width and height of the book. You can find all of them at the link in the endnotes.3

Ingram Spark

Ingram Spark (IS) is the indie author branch of Lightning Source, an international company that has been serving the publishing industry for fifty years. By printing through IS, an indie author can access the same distribution network as traditional publishers. IS also provides the ability to do hardcover books by POD.

With a similar process to KDP's, IS is often the next step for new authors after KDP. If you are planning on adding IS in the future, I recommend choosing a trim size that you can use in both places. Many, but not all, are the same on both platforms.

IS is not recommended for e-books, although they offer that as an option. Their expertise and platform are best for print books.

If you first publish with KDP and then wish to add IS, open an account with IS and then ask them to transfer your title. They will assist you in the current process. Currently it consists of filling out a form, and then they import all your files. Do not create a title for the book, they will do so for you.

---

3   https://kdp.amazon.com/en_US/help/topic/G201834180.

Going Wide with eBooks

Distributors

You can go with multiple places for wide distribution of your books. You can target many world-wide marketplaces through aggregators such as Draft2Digital, Publish Drive, Streetlib, and Smashwords. You can go directly to Google Play, Barnes & Noble, Apple, and Kobo. These are the four largest marketplaces outside of Amazon as of this writing. The markets the aggregators serve change, so I won't go into that here. You'll want to research current agreements and information when you're ready to make that decision.

You'll want to consider how many places you want to upload to. If you choose many, I recommend using some kind of form or check sheet so that you can keep the places organized. I adapted the Upload Check Sheet on page 54 from what I used for a recent series.

If you are not going direct, then the aggregator will take a cut of the royalties you receive from the platforms where they push your book. You may prefer that slight cut to uploading manually yourself to many places.

All of these platforms will allow preorders except for KDP print. If you're doing a preorder, then you will need to go back and upload your KDP print files once the book is live.

I do not use Draft2Digital, because when I went wide, PublishDrive distributed everywhere they do plus many others. However, PD has changed how they pay their royalties, so I would encourage you to go with D2D instead as PD is no longer user-friendly for beginner authors.

Also, when I went wide, Google Play was difficult to manage direct as was Apple. I understand this has changed recently, but I have not pulled my books from PD to go direct as of yet. I'll probably do that shortly. Although you can change later, part of my problem is the number of books that I have written—nearly thirty!—that I must move, so it takes more time now than if I had started there.

Most people first use D2D when going wide. You'll hit all the major retailers that way, and they're a great company to work with from all I've heard.

Audio

The audio book format is growing in popularity among readers and profitability for authors. Amazon also has an exclusive platform that you can go through, or you can release on other platforms without exclusivity contracts.

Audio is on my list of things to do, but I haven't released audiobooks yet, so I will leave this subject to those with more experience than I. I recommend Audio for Authors by Bradley Charbonneau4 and Audio for Authors by Joanna Penn5–links in the endnotes.

---

4   Audio for Authors by Bradley Charbonneau: https://books2read.com/u/bzg5Jq
5   Audio for Authors by Joanna Penn: https://books2read.com/u/4A7ZGo

CHAPTER THREE

Text vs Image

Text based books

Text-based books are just like what the phrase says: nearly all text with few if any images. Genres include most fiction from middle grade on up and nonfiction with few charts, images, etc. If you have a text-based book, skip to the next chapter for research. If you have some images in your book, the information in the image-based section will apply to you.

Image Based ➡️

Image based books

Image-based books include children's picture books, cookbooks, and art books. I would also include nonfiction that relies heavily on charts, graphs, screenshots, or other image-based content.

In the next section, you'll do some research on specifics for your categories and hopefully decide which trim size is best for what you want to do. Right now, I want you to understand a bit why that decision is especially important if you are including images in your books.

I'll review some terms and their meanings. Bleed is an extra amount outside of the trim size of the book. It is used when you want the image to go to the edge of the page. It is typically 0.125" on all sides except the interior edge or margin where the book is bound, otherwise known as the gutter. This allows for any slight errors in printing so you don't have a white line on the edge of your page.

In order for an image to print well, it needs to be 300 ppi or pixels per inch. This means that the image must be 300 pixels for every inch that the image will be in the book. You will need to include the bleed in that amount. For example, my children's books are 8x10, so the size of the image needs to be 8.125 x 10.25. (8 + bleed) x (10 + bleed twice). You can then multiply those numbers by 300 to get 2438 x 3075 pixels. This is a minimum number. As you can see, the trim size plays a critical role here.

If you are commissioning artwork, I recommend giving the illustrator a slightly larger format to work from, such as 9x11 for an 8x10 book, but let them know they should not put anything important on the outside one inch or so. They will have more flexibility when formatting your book so that you have a sufficiently large image.

If the illustrator is working analog and plans to scan in the work or if you are using scans or images of your artwork or of other photographs, including screenshots, you will want to ensure that the resulting jpg images are at least 300 ppi at the size you want to use them. I prefer starting from larger and going to smaller, and then I compress the images when exporting the final files.

Also note, that for POD, any color means that your book will be in full color for printing purposes. This increases the cost of production, which is passed on to you. There is no such thing as spot color in POD—it's all or nothing. So full-spread images will cost the same as small color changes in text. In my opinion, go big or go home with the color as long as you do it tastefully.

Research
Rest Area

Research

I HAVE A PRE-TRIP Preparation PDF at the end of this chapter that you can use to collect the information I discuss below when you do your research. Use whatever will be easy for you to refer back to later. I also suggest you grab the Marketing PDF. I'm not going to go into marketing in this book as I still have too much to learn about that. But what I do know is that much of the same research that you will find helpful in publishing your book will be useful to you when you market. I wish I had known this sooner.

I want you to do your research based on the categories you plan to use for your book. Do note that the categories are not necessarily the same for e-book and print for some genres, so make a note of those differences as you go along. Why should you do this? You want readers to be able to find your book. So you want your book to sit on the same shelf as similar books so that people who are interested in those books will see your book, pick it up, and hopefully fall in love. Your cover will help your book look like it fits, so make sure that the insides match the outside. Disappointed readers do not leave happy reviews, so make sure you are fulfilling your promise to your reader.

You can do research on Amazon, Goodreads, and Barnes & Noble, or perhaps Kobo if you are Canadian and expect that to be a major market for you. You don't want to spend months on this, but you want to do enough research to have a solid feel for the trends or to know that this isn't actually the right fit for your book. While disappointing, that's actually very helpful information.

Use as many of the sheets as you like, but keep each category on a separate page or pages. Write the title and subtitle of the book. Not all books have subtitles, so make a note of that. You may see trends appear. For example, punny titles are quintessentially cozy mystery. You often find long subtitles in nonfiction books. This information will help you conform to what's typical for books in your genre.

Remember, trim size is the size of the print version of the book. Even if you're not planning on doing a print version, make a note of this information in case you change your mind later. Depending on genre, print books are still popular with readers.

Book length is listed as the number of pages in the details of the book. Price is obvious. Something not so obvious is the other categories that the book may be listed in. This may give you a better idea of what categories you should use.

Also, take a screenshot of the top fifty to one hundred titles in each of your categories. This will help you understand what kind of covers people are looking for. I'll discuss that more in the cover design section, but you should address this while you're there as that will help you and save you time later.

Again, in all this, you are looking for trends. You want to know what's typical for your categories so you can better succeed in all your efforts.

A Simple Route to Publishing
Pre-Trip Preparation

Category: _____

Gather information from the bestsellers in your categories.
Take screen shots of the covers of the top 100, you'll want them later.

Title: _____   Title: _____

Subtitle: _____   Subtitle: _____

Trim Size: _____   Trim Size: _____

Length: _____   Length: _____

Price: _____   Price: _____

Other Categories: Other Categories:

_____   _____

_____   _____

Title: _____   Title: _____

Subtitle: _____   Subtitle: _____

Trim Size: _____   Trim Size: _____

Length: _____   Length: _____

Price: _____   Price: _____

Other Categories: Other Categories:

_____   _____

_____   _____

A Simple Route to Publishing
Marketing Research Checklist

PUBLISHING
Indie Route
101

Author	Website	Podcast	Class	FB	IG	LI	TW	Other

CHAPTER FIVE

Editing

E DITING MAY BE the bane of most people's existence and can be the most expensive part of the publishing process. This depends on what level of editing you need and on how long your book is.

I often see people asking how much it will cost to edit a book. That's like asking how long a piece of string is.

The answer is, it depends.

The most common forms of editing include developmental, line edits, and copy edits in order of comprehensiveness and expense. Proofreading is a final review of the book.

A developmental edit refers to the overall organization and structure of the book. This will vary, depending on if you're working with fiction or nonfiction. Here, you are addressing the big picture and overall content of your book. Does the book flow and make sense?

A line or copy edit are not exactly the same, but the terms are sometimes used interchangeably. Line editing includes minor rewrites and the clarification of awkward wording. Copy editing is what you typically think of when someone says "editing": the correction of grammar, typos, spelling, and punctuation.

Proofreading can happen at several points along the publishing path but comes after editing and often after formatting to catch any errors in either the words or the formatting of the book. This is right before uploading.

You will typically need to pay and/or barter for these services. Yes, bartering is alive and well in the indie sphere!

Choosing an Editor

How do you choose an editor? Ask around for recommendations. You want someone competent in your genre who knows the Chicago Manual of Style (CMoS as you'll see it often) if you are in the US. That's the acceptable style manual for published books. A retired English teacher may or may not have the skills necessary if they are not familiar with the most up-to-date CMoS rules.

Cost

The cost of editing generally depends on how much work your manuscript needs. Thus, I recommend first doing as much self and friend editing as possible. People sometimes want to skip editing due to the expense. I'll do all that I can in order to send as clean a manuscript as possible to my editor. You should especially do this if you do not choose to hire a professional editor. However, I cannot recommend a professional edit enough, but I understand if it's not possible.

How can you effectively polish your manuscript as much as possible?

Use tools, such as ProWritingAid. Grammarly is another option, but I don't recommend it as my editor and many of her colleagues avoid it. The user must be very familiar with the rules of grammar, so it might not be effective for new authors who are unsure of these rules. Spell check in your word processor is also helpful.

Ask friends or other writers in your genre to do a beta read of your book. This is often before the pro editing step, as fresh eyes will help you identify weak points in your manuscript and find many typos. The best beta readers would be in your target audience for the book, those interested in your topic or who typically read your genre.

My friend Katherine Walden wrote this book, which I also recommend: Insider Editing tips for Self-Publishers: Avoiding Embarrassing Typos and Grammatical Errors6. It will be an excellent resource for you.

---

6   Insider Editing tips for Self-Publishers: Avoiding Embarrassing Typos and Grammatical Errors by Katherine Walden: https://books2read.com/u/b5kyz6

CHAPTER SIX

Formatting

E-BOOKS FUNCTION MUCH like a website does, as one continuous flow of text, unless you use a non-reflowable version. But if you've read a novel or most nonfiction on an e-reader, you've experienced the reflowable e-book. The reader can set the font and size of text among other features, so the author has less control over the final appearance of the book.

Children's books and other image-heavy books are typically in non-reflowable format. However, this can limit your readers as this format doesn't work well on all e-reader devices.

The table of contents is hyperlinked to the various chapters so you can easily navigate through the book.

EPub and mobi files are the most commonly used file formats. Mobi is KDP's proprietary file format but recently announced they would only accept EPubs. EPub is used everywhere else.

Done for you

You can hire someone to do e-book formatting, or you can use templates or online formatters, such as D2D's or Reedsy's. Scrivener will export an e-book for you. If you will be publishing multiple books, look into Vellum. It's built for Macs, but if you have a PC, you can use Mac in Cloud to run it.

If you are going with KDP and doing image-based books, Kindle Kid's Book Creator is easy to use and works well.

I use InDesign for all my formatting, which is the industry standard, but it's probably overkill for general publishing by an author.

DIY

I find formatting for print a more enjoyable, though arguably more tedious task. It's the artist in me, but I love having a beautifully laid-out book. Since your book will be in print, what you choose is what it will look like in the final product.

Some terms you'll come across include:

Margin: This is probably what you think, the space around the top, outside, and bottom of your page. As I previously mentioned, the minimums for KDP are 0.25", but I recommend a larger margin, especially for the outside edge, so the reader's thumb has some space to hold the book without covering text.

Gutter: This is the space on the inside edge of the page so the left-hand side of a right-hand page and vice versa. The minimum varies based on the number of pages in your book. You can find details on this space for KDP here: https://kdp.amazon.com/en_US/help/topic/G202145400. Again, I recommend increasing those amounts to make it easy for the reader to read.

Bleed: As previously mentioned, this is typically 0.125" beyond the margins of the page. They use it for images that go to the edge. You take the image beyond the edge so that any variance in printing will not result in a white line. They trim this extra space off before they bind the book.

Trim size: This is the width and height of your book, commonly 6x9 for nonfiction books. This means that the book is 6 inches wide and 9 inches tall.

Spine width: This is the width of the spine. This depends on the number of pages and the color of the paper. Cream paper is slightly thicker than white paper, and though slight, this difference adds up quickly and will result in an error if you've used one to calculate the spine width (or downloaded a template, which I recommend) but selected the other when uploading your files.

Vellum: This is a popular way to format your books for print and e-book. D2D is developing a print formatter that is in beta stages at the time of this writing. People also format using Word or Scrivener. I use InDesign, but you might not want to deal with the fairly steep learning curve. Affinity Publisher is a comparable tool to InDesign for a one time payment.

COVER
DESIGN

CHAPTER SEVEN

Cover Design

A BOOK COVER CAN make or break the financial success of your book. It is the first thing that people see, and they will judge your book by its cover.

Your book cover has one purpose: to sell your book. It is the primary advertisement for what lies between the pages. It need not describe or be representational of the contents, but it should give potential readers a strong indication of what they will find inside. You want the right readers—not just any reader—to see your book. To do that, you need to meet the reader's expectations. The cover needs to be consistent with the content of the book.

Genre Consistent

People categorize and notice similarities and differences. The wise author uses this to their advantage. Look at books in your genre or any genre. Notice that they have a similar feel, similar colors, consistency in types of imagery, and similar font choices. In some genres, you see very few differences between one cover and the next.

You want to stand out from the crowd, but not too much. Your book needs to look like it fits on the shelf next to the others in your genre. This similarity tells your reader that they will most likely enjoy this book. Give the reader what they want; this leads to excellent reviews and repeat buyers.

Series Branding

If you have a series of books, you want to tighten up the similarities of your covers even more. You want people to recognize at a glance that those books belong together. You brand a series by using covers which are very similar as to imagery, fonts, and layout.

Overall Design

Your design needs to be cohesive with a clear focal point. The reader's eyes should immediately go to where you want them to focus, typically on your title or on one part of the image. Beware of trying to put too much on the cover. You have about three seconds to capture the reader's attention. Once you have their interest, you can hook them with the description and/or back cover copy. If the reader doesn't know where to look, they will scroll on by.

Check the Thumbnail

People purchase most books online in marketplaces, such as Amazon. The reader's first encounter with your book will be the cover at thumbnail size, which is almost microscopic. How your cover design holds up at the thumbnail size is an important consideration. Most successful authors and designers will tell you that your title and image must be discernible, even at thumbnail size. Some disagree as that information is right next to the image, but their opinion is in the minority.

Crowd Sourcing

Crowd-sourcing opinions on your cover can be helpful. Other eyes can spot issues you've missed. But these can also mislead you and contradict each other, especially if the commenters are not familiar with, or readers of, your genre. What appeals to a reader of sweet romance will differ from what appeals to readers of thrillers. You need to know who your readers are, which is as important as knowing what they like.

Research

Remember the screenshots you took of the best sellers in your categories? It's time to take them back out and see what trends or similarities you find. Look for colors, types of images, typefaces or fonts used, or other elements consistent across the best sellers in your genre.

Cover trends can change over time, so you might want to do this every couple of years, depending on your genre. Some genres change more quickly than others, so you should check periodically to see if you need to refresh your covers. If your sales are dipping more than you think they should, evaluate your cover. It isn't the only reason for declining sales, but it can be one of them.

In this section, I'll cover some strategies to do it yourself, although as a designer, I have to say that this rarely goes as well as I hoped. We're too close to our own work, and cover design needs a fairly comprehensive skill set. An amateur cover will negatively affect sales. But depending on your reasons for publishing, this may not matter to you.

For example, you might not worry as much about a genre-appropriate cover if you are publishing something for friends and family, if you have a platform that will buy it regardless, or if you're giving away books as gifts or for free promotion. If your name or position will sell the book, then the cover is less critical to its success. I would also add that if you are the only book or one of a few on the topic, the cover may not affect sales as much as if you have a lot of competition.

If you are marketing to a broader, more general audience, the cover will need to be on point. Although there are exceptions, this is the prevailing wisdom of many successful authors.

Interestingly, indies are leaping ahead of traditional publishing in this area. Traditional publishing relies on advertising dollars to sell books, somewhat as a brute-force attack. Many indies make much more than traditional authors, and they know that a cover that meets genre expectations will help them sell their book, so they will ensure that it does just that.

Design Basics for DIY

Both KDP and IS have templates to ensure that you get the size of the cover correct. These are based on the trim size, the number of pages, and the color of the paper that you are using. Again, while it seems like it should be insignificant, the color of the paper matters. Cream paper is slightly thicker than white and that difference adds up in a hurry. This is the number one reason for errors when uploading your book, so use your Directions for the Journey Form on page 48 and make a note of the color of paper you'll be using and stay with that.

It is best to stick with two fonts only for a book cover. Font pairing is an art form in and of itself. You can do an online search for "font pairing" and the year, and look through the results to find a pair that seems to fit your categories and the feel of your book. Be sure that the font you are choosing is available and appropriately licensed for commercial (as opposed to personal) use.

You should buy stock images from a paid site, not a free one. Free stock sites do not vet the images and leave you open to potential copyright and trademark infringements. There are many levels of copyright and potential trademark issues that you need to avoid, and the easiest way to do that is to purchase your stock through Deposit Photo, Shutterstock, or a similar site that offers some guarantee and protection to you should they mistakenly allow an image subject to copyright or trademark law. Even a brief scan of free stock sites shows many images that infringe on copyright and trademark and other image restrictions.

What would happen if you used an image incorrectly? It all depends, but the least troubling thing that could happen would be that you would need to take down your book and change the cover. You could be fined or sued for large sums of money. I'm not extremely risk averse, but this seems like an easily avoided hassle to just do it right the first time.

On the cover template for KDP or Ingram Spark, you'll notice that lines show where the cover will fold and safe zones. Print on demand is not as precise of a printing process as off-set printing, so they have built in those tolerances to their templates. Be aware of those as you are planning your design.

I typically use a combination of Photoshop and InDesign, but I've heard people use Canva and Gimp. From what I understand, Canva has book cover templates, but I have not used them, so I don't know how that works. Some find Affinity Photo and Affinity Designer to be good alternatives for Photoshop and Illustrator which are available for a one time fee instead of a subscription.

Two books with more helpful in-depth information are Book Cover Design Secrets by Derek Murphy[7] and The Author's Guide to Cover Design by Stuart Bache[8].

---

7   Book Cover Design Secrets by Derek Murphy https://books2read.com/u/mVgEoA

8   The Author's Guide to Cover Design by Stuart Bache: https://books2read.com/u/3JXdQg

SD

I mentioned premade covers earlier. This is an excellent starting point if budget is an issue. Many authors begin with a cover that they can afford and then upgrade later if they find that sales are not as strong for the book as they would like. You can change your cover whenever you wish and upload new files.

Premade covers work because of the proven principle that it is more important to nail down genre than to be a perfect description of your book. So designers can create designs that fulfill genre expectations without a specific book in mind. Many authors find these are great story starters.

Premade covers are an effective way to get a professionally designed book cover for much less. You can typically change your name, tagline, and title or any other important information on the cover without further fees. Altering the design itself may or may not be available and may come with extra fees.

Some designers are also doing what they call custom premades. These are still much less than a custom book cover, and the designer takes your information to inform their design choices. However, unlike a custom design, the resulting cover is a take-it or leave-it item once completed. When available, these are an excellent value for both the author and the designer.

If you have any questions about what is or is not allowed with either a premade or a custom premade, ask your designer before purchasing. Be aware that designers are professionals, and you are paying for their knowledge and experience, not just their time.

Custom

Potentially the most expensive, but arguably the best value for your time and money is a professional cover design. Ask for recommendations for designers from others in your genre/categories. Do your due diligence and look at their portfolios. A website is a sign that the person takes their business seriously and would be a point in their favor. Cover design is a booming industry and not everyone who calls themselves a designer knows what's required or is a true professional.

The designer is your partner in creating a book cover that will attract the right eyes to your book. Treat them with respect and communicate what you want before you begin and during the design process. Also remember that the designer is working to provide you with the best possible cover to help sell your book, so if they push back on your ideas or desires for changes, consider their suggestions carefully.

So where do you start? The place to start is with your book. Remember the research that you did early on with your categories? Here's another place where this research will save you lots of time and frustration. The genre or categories of your book will help you narrow down your choices for book cover designers. You can Google to find a smaller range of designers or ask for recommendations in genre-based Facebook groups. Once you've found a few who work in your genre, check out their portfolios. Do they show a strong understanding of your genre? Every artist has a style, but is the designer able to adapt to the needs of the book and author they are working with? If you see books by various authors in that designer's portfolio that look as if they are in the same series, I recommend that you go no further. The designer's job is to make your book look like you, not others. This is part of branding, and you want your unique brand, not the designer's. If your genre calls for photographic covers and the designer has only illustrations, you'll want to look elsewhere.

Once you find one with the look you're going for, then check out their terms and conditions and about pages. Do they sound like someone you could work with? Do you feel that they will get your project? Do you have common ground with the designer? You will work better with some designers than others; that's often a personality match or conflict rather than a skill level. You need to communicate well with the designer and he or she with you for the best experience possible.

Do they have information on their turnaround times and/or scheduling availability, and will that fit with your schedule? Turnaround times for a premade cover are usually quick and may be a perfect option for you, so head back to that section. Custom covers require additional time and communication back and forth. This is often reflected in the price points of those packages. Most designers work on covers in the order in which they were hired, so check with the designer on their timeframe to be sure it will fit your schedule.

In your initial communications with your chosen designer, be clear in your expectations about the process and your cover. Hopefully, the designer has made their expectations clear on their site, and yours matches them well. If you've worked with other designers, let them know what worked well and what didn't. This hopefully goes without saying, but be respectful. Your designer is a highly skilled professional and should be treated as such.

I haven't mentioned price. It probably goes without saying as this is the piece that most of us are the most acutely aware of. But price, within reason, is a secondary concern. In some ways, you get what you pay for, but in others, it's irrelevant. A $2000 sci-fi cover will not help sell your self-help book—nor would it if you spent multiples of that! It's just the wrong cover for the book.

Some designers, like myself, have various tiers of packages for design so you can choose one that best fits your book and your budget. We are your partners in this venture and want you and your book to do well. While the cover is not the only determinant of the success of your book, it is your readers' first exposure to your book.

A word of caution about sites with cheap designers and sites where the designers compete for your job. You can find some excellent designers and strong designs on such sites, but you should also be aware of potential legal risks. As the author, you will be culpable for any fines if the designer chooses images or fonts that are not licensed for commercial purposes or if they do not have the appropriate releases signed.

Information to Give to Your Designer

Your designer will need to know the following for a custom book design:

1. The genre and categories you will put your book in
2. The tone of your book
3. A synopsis of your book and any key elements. Hold these loosely, though. It is far more important that your book cover nail the genre/category than depict your exact story.
4. Samples of covers in your category(ies) that you like and why you like them. Do you like the feel, the colors, the typography, the placement of the text or other elements, the type of image, etc.? This helps your designer get a feel for what you like and what you think will work well. They may push back and make other recommendations based on their experience. Again, your designer wants your book to succeed as that's also a measure of how well they do their job. You may overrule them, but consider their points carefully before doing so.

Print

If you will be also adding print edition(s),

1. Are you doing softcover/paperback or hardcover or both?
2. What is the total number of formatted pages in your book?
3. What color paper will you be using? Nearly all uploading errors of print covers occur because the author told the designer one color and selected another when uploading the files. Amazon and IS will kick your file back because the spine size will be incorrect.
4. What do you want on the back cover as to blurb, bio, photo, etc.? Keep in mind you have a finite amount of space.
5. What is the book's trim size?

Legal Considerations

People don't usually address the legalities of a book cover, and yet if you are unaware of potential legal issues, you could find yourself in a huge mess. I am not a lawyer, and the following does not constitute legal advice—just a friendly heads up of some issues to be aware of. If you have specific questions, seek the advice of a lawyer in your area familiar with the law related to publication.

By default, the artist or designer—the same as an author—holds the copyright for their creations. Unless you have a contract that says otherwise, you do not own the cover of your book; the designer does. Neither of you would own the images within that design unless you created them. In effect, the creator of the image and the designer licenses their images to you for use on your book cover. It is generally understood that the image will also be used in promotional materials, so those are covered, but check with your designer to be sure.

Images and Artwork

For stock images, most standard licenses come with a set number of imprints (e.g., copies of your book) that it can be used on. If sales of your book go over that number, then you must purchase an extended license. This is typically a rather large number, so if you exceed it, you can rejoice and be glad you require the extended license. The precise number varies depending on where the image is licensed, so check the fine print wherever you find your image. The responsibility of appropriate licensing falls with you, the author, so make sure your designer is pulling images from a reliable source.

If your image has people in it, then model releases are also required. Reputable stock image sites will note if a model release is on file and what, if any, limitations there are. Again, this is your responsibility. If the use of their image is not according to their contract, you can be sued by the model, and they will most likely win. Ignorance of the law does not excuse you.

Also, beware of any images that include copyrighted or trademarked elements. For example, if someone is dressed as Minnie Mouse and someone takes their photo, the photographer and model may give their consent, but Disney most likely has not. The same would be true of brand names, logos, etc. Again, the burden of the law falls on you as the image is on something you have published. Incidentally, this is true regardless of if the image is on a for-sale product or not. You must adhere to copyright and trademark laws and licensing on your blog as well as on the cover of your book.

Designer

When the designer takes the images, your title, and your author name and compiles them into the cover image for your book, that compilation is by default under their copyright by law. Unless stated otherwise in your contract, you cannot legally change that image in any way or use the image for anything other than its intended purpose. If you need changes, contact the designer, who will make them for you.

The reasons for this are very complex and relate to the use of stock images. This is a gray area, so many reputable designers will err on the side of caution and not give you source files, only finished ones. The artistic reason is that a book's cover design is a carefully crafted piece of art, and undue tinkering will destroy the balance and effectiveness of the design.

Work-for-Hire

Work-for-hire is an exception to the copyright law that the designer or creator owns the copyright to their creation. Work-for-hire can occur in the context of an employee creating work within the scope of their employment. That probably doesn't apply to you, the self-published author. The other exception is when a freelance artist and the client both sign an agreement stating that the work is for hire, and it falls under one of the following nine categories:

- A contribution to a collective work
- A contribution used as part of a motion picture or other audio-visual work
- A supplementary work, which includes pictorial illustrations, maps, and charts, done to supplement a work by another author
- A compilation
- A translation
- An atlas
- A test
- Answer material for a test
- An instructional text (defined as a literary, pictorial, or graphic work prepared for publication and with the purpose of use in systematic instructional activities)

Anything outside of these nine categories cannot be considered work-for-hire with or without a signed contract. 9

9   Artists Guild Graphic, The Graphic Artists Guild Handbook Pricing & Ethical
    Guidelines, 14th Ed. (New York: Artists Guild Graphic, 2013), 33–34.

CHAPTER EIGHT

Meta Data

O N THE DIRECTIONS for Your Journey Page (p 48) is the metadata that you'll need when you upload your book onto whatever sites you've chosen. The form assumes one pen name and publisher imprint. If you are using an additional imprint or pen name, you might wish to make a note of those.

Metadata is all the behind-the-scenes information that lets the distributors know what kind of book it is and who might be interested in it. Their search engines pay particular attention to the title, subtitle, categories, and keywords. These should be self-explanatory.

Release date is included for future reference and if you are planning a pre-order so you can ensure that date is the same everywhere you upload your book.

ISBN refers to the International Standard Book Number. It is a unique identifier for each format of your book. There is one provider of these per country, and some of you are lucky enough to get them free. Most e-book retailers assign their own numbers, so some people do not use an ISBN for their e-book. Paperback, hardback, and audio will need their own. Both KDP and IS offer free ISBNs, but they belong to those platforms, and it will show them as the publisher of record. It may also confuse libraries and potential readers if they see are two numbers for the same thing. After you've purchased them, you will need to assign an ISBN to each format of your book.

Bowker is the place to purchase ISBNs in the U.S. and Neilson is for the U.K. Canada, France, and South Africa provide them for free for their citizens. Other places selling ISBNs, or giving them away, like KDP and IS have purchased them in bulk, which reduces the price, from the appropriate place in that country and are reselling them.

The description is the sales copy or blurb for your book. This text will sell the book to potential readers once the cover has caught their eye. You can use the Kindlepreneur Book Description Generator10 to attractively format your description and then paste that into the field at KDP.

Keywords are not just single words but phrases that people might search for to find your book. You have seven available to you in most places.

Categories are where you can drill down to the best niche for your book. Remember the market research you did before? Use that information to help guide your choices here. The categories for print and e-book

---

10 https://kindlepreneur.com/amazon-book-description-generator/

are slightly different, so this is a great way to increase your discoverability by choosing different but still applicable categories.

If you know what your prices will be, you can make a note of them before you begin. If not, both IS and KDP have suggested prices and/or calculators that show the potential profit at the price points you choose to help you decide. Some people adjust prices for a specific profit per book; others prefer consistent pricing. Again, refer to the research you did earlier to assist you in these choices. Your price is not locked in, so you can adjust this later if you desire.

A Simple Route to Publishing
Directions for the Journey

Title: _____

Subtitle: _____

Author Name: _____

Imprint: _____

Series & Number: _____

Release Date: _____

ISBNs

eBook: _____ Paperback: _____

Hardback: _____ Audio: _____

Description: _____
_____
_____
_____
_____
_____
_____

Keywords (7): _____
_____
_____
_____

Ebook Categories: _____
_____

Print Categories: _____
_____

Age Range (Children's Books): _____

Trim Size: _____ Paper Color: _____

Ebook Price: _____ Paperback Price: _____

Hardback Price: _____ Audio Price: _____

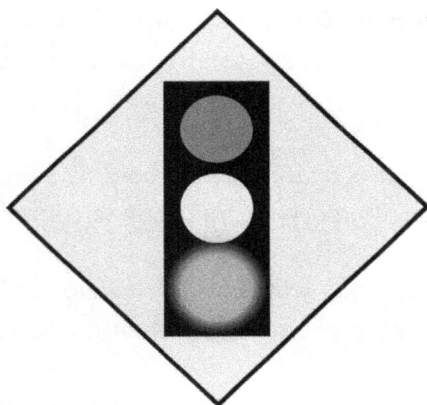

CHAPTER NINE

Publish

Y OU WILL NEED to create accounts where you wish to upload
your book. I have found this to always be a straightforward process. You will need to have your bank account and tax information
handy. That will vary, depending on your legal status as a person or a
company, etc., so I can't advise you on specifics. I created most of my

accounts a few years ago, so the process may have changed since then. If you become stuck or confused, a search will be helpful.

You will also need to determine what account you wish your royalties deposited into. As far as I know, this must be a checking account at a bank. Some international authors use other services as an intermediary. You can ask in author groups or do an online search to find what works best in your country.

You can do this step whenever you like. If you have time while waiting on editors or cover designers, feel free to get this step out of the way.

Upload

Once you set up your account(s), your book is edited and formatted, your cover is designed, and your metadata is compiled, you are ready to upload your files.

On each platform, you will want to create or add a new title. Each platform requires largely the same information, just not always in the same order.

Some additional questions that you may come across as you upload ask if the book is in the public domain and if you have worldwide rights. If you've written this book and you have not sold or given any rights away, the answer to the first is no and the second is yes. Books in the public domain are those out of copyright (in the US, seventy-five years after the death of the author). In traditional realms, a publisher typically allowed the author to keep the rights to other geographical areas in addition to their primary market.

Your "Directions for the Journey" worksheet will be your guide. Fill in the information as you go along. All platforms have a verification or quality control process that your files will need to go through before the book will be live. I would also recommend purchasing a proof copy of your print books to make sure they look like you think they will. This is also a great time to do a final proofread as your mind will see the book differently in a new form.

When you and the platform are satisfied with your files, you can hit the publish button and then wait for your book to show up on the platform.

If you have published print with KDP and are adding Ingram Spark, speak to a representative for a file transfer. See p. 15 for more.

Royalties

When will you receive the royalties from books sold?

KDP pays sixty days after the end of the month in which the book was sold or the pages read for those in KU.

IS pays ninety days after the book is sold.

Other platforms will have information on the frequency and requirements of their payouts.

When you run ads, remember that you will not see the earnings for a while, but the platforms will want to be paid the same month as you run the ads.

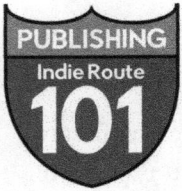

A Simple Route to Publishing
Upload Checksheet

Book Title: _____

Interior:

☐ ePub

☐ mobi

☐ PDF - interior

Cover:

☐ ebook cover

☐ KDP cover

☐ IS cover

Platforms

☐ KDP

☐ IS

☐ Payhip

☐ Website

☐ Kobo

☐ PublishDrive

☐ Smashwords

☐ Streetlib

☐ KDP print (once preorder is live)

CHAPTER TEN

Marketing

CONGRATULATIONS! YOU'VE PUBLISHED your book and completed this leg of your journey! The next leg of that journey is marketing. I am not an expert, and what works depends on so many factors that I can't advise you. I suggest that you look at the 20Booksto50K® Facebook group. Their files contain reams of great information and advice. They are helpful but don't take kindly to people who don't do their own search of the files, as so many questions you'll have are amply answered there.

You will find Facebook groups for nearly any genre of writing that you can think of, so check them out to find helpful people.

IndieAuthorTools.com is a new website with lots of information and tools to use on your journey.

Resources

You can find links to great resources for the rest of your Indie Route Journey at the link below. Enjoy your journey!
https://kingdomcovers.com/indie-route-resources

Author Note

If my counting is correct, I've published or been a contributor to the content of thirty books, including this one. I'm also a designer for book covers and interiors and work with a lot of first-time authors. This book started as a way to answer all the questions that those authors had and that I had myself when I was starting out, so I completely understand. I hope you find it helpful, and that it helps you not become overwhelmed with the process.

I also love to garden, and even though it's January, I'll be starting my tender plants so they'll be ready to put out in the garden once the danger of frost is past. I'll be planting the cold hardy vegetables, such as lettuce, peas, and potatoes, outside. I've only been on this property for a few years, and I'm still figuring out how and what to grow here.

Having a productive garden depends on the sun, the rain—or irrigation here in Texas—the soil, and the seed. For optimal results, all aspects need to be within the preferences for what you're trying to grow. But no matter how perfect the situation is, growing a garden is still a lot of work.

Publishing a book is a lot like that: a lot of factors and a lot of work. But it's all worth it when you hold that final product in your hand.

I hope you persevere through the work and all the many moving parts of the process so that you can continue to move forward until you reap the rewards of your book published.

Enjoy the wonderful adventure of your publishing journey!
Alice

PART 4

Real Estate Deal Acquisition Secrets

What No One Is Telling You About Acquiring A Consistent Flow of
Real Estate Deals

Jerome Lewis

Foreword

I F YOU'RE LOOKING for practical, professional advice on how to generate real estate deals, then this is the book for you. In these pages, you'll find everything you need to know in order to be successful in this arena.

From finding the right properties to marketing them effectively, we'll cover all the bases and give you the secrets to Real Estate Acquisition Success.

So whether you're a beginner or a seasoned pro, this book will have something for you. So let's get started and learn all the secrets to real estate acquisition success!Preface

If you're looking for practical, professional advice on how to generate real estate deals, then this is the book for you.

In these pages, you'll find exactly what you need to know in order to be successful with generating real estate deals consistently — **NOT** some overnight pop-up operation that will have you constantly thirsting for business.

The strategies discussed here will show you how to employ a system that will bring you _consistent_ deals.

From finding the right properties to marketing them effectively, we'll cover all the bases and give you the secrets to *Real Estate Deal Acquisition Success.*

So whether you're a beginner or a seasoned pro, this book will have something for you. So let's get started and learn all the secrets to real estate acquisition success!

Introduction

F ELLOW REAL ESTATE Entrepreneur,
   Setting up your Deal Acquisition Strategy can be an over-
   whelming and frustrating experience.
Why?

Because we're inundated with so many marketing messages (accord-ing to Forbes.com it's up to 10,000 a day) and you're bound to feel overwhelmed and even misled when it comes to finding someone you can trust.

With confusing lead processes, super-high commission splits, bad service, confusing tech systems all too common, making a wise decision is more important than ever.

This is Jerome and here at Digital Real Estate Strategy. We help real estate agents, real estate entrepreneurs, and real estate investors like you take charge of their marketing even if you hate technology.

And I want to take away any fears, frustration, or confusion as you go through this process. That's why I created this book, entitled:

Deal Acquisition Frustration Elimination

INSIDE YOU WILL discover exactly what you need to know so that you can make an informed decision about choosing the right deal acquisition strategy for you.

It's been designed in a simple, easy-to-understand way, so you can experience predictable results – that you want and deserve.

Okay, let's get started!

CHAPTER 1

Why Should You Listen To Me?

M Y NAME IS Jerome Lewis. The silly, serious, and introverted Millennial from Philadelphia, PA. Getting sent through different foster homes and being raised by a single mother helped me to understand the significance of family. I am a father and family man. I have worked jobs ranging from retail, customer service, and even IT/tech. I left my job in "Corporate America" for the pursuit of entrepreneurship. More specifically real estate entrepreneurship. It was always a dream of mine to "work for myself."

As a real estate entrepreneur, I have varying experiences within the real estate industry. Real estate investing, real estate events, real estate coaching, real estate agency. This is important to you because I have been in your place before. I have felt your pain, aggravation, and confusion. When you got into this business, you had huge aspirations of wealth and financial success — all fueled by real estate. You do this not only for yourself...but for those close to you, especially your family. Having worked with and shared stages with some of the industry's top real estate agents, real estate investors, and real estate coaches, I understand the exact frustrations that take place within the real estate industry.

In many instances, we have chosen real estate as a career because we see how those huge transactions can get us closer to the financial freedom we've always dreamed about.

In our mind, real estate wasn't just one way. It was the *best* way. And if you're still reading this, you still feel this way. I'm here to say, what you feel is still true. Real estate is still one of the best ways to build wealth and propel you, your family, and your loved ones to that financial freedom you know are within your grasp.

You've learned all the cool "tricks and strategies," such as "wholesaling, creative financing, listing strategies, open houses, and more." You're working hard, chugging away, prospecting, cold calling, using social media, text blasting, SMS messaging, building relationships, etc. But for some reason, it's still not giving you your ultimate goal of more consistent deals/transactions closed.

I promise you, the way you achieve the consistency you desire in your real estate business is by effective marketing and lead generation. I have been in your position before. I have asked the same questions that you are asking and I have had the same struggles as you. I understand exactly how you feel when you are continually met with frustration and confusion. Whether you are a real estate agent, real estate investor, real estate coach, or you run another relevant real estate business — lead generation and marketing are vital to your success. It is my personal mission to help you eliminate frustration and get clear on what you need to do so you can achieve success in your business.

Okay, now that you know a little about me let's get into what you need to know to take charge of your deal acquisition strategy.

CHAPTER 2

Closed Deals Come From Leads

W HAT DOES THIS mean?
Closed deals from leads. Leads come from your marketing strategy and your marketing strategy must include lead generation.

Most "gurus" are telling you straight-up <u>lies</u> with nonsense phrases like these:

"Call up your sphere and the deals will come rolling in."

"Tell everyone what you do and they'll tell everyone and you'll be successful in no time."

"Just call FSBO and add value."

But you know just like I know, it's not that simple.

The bottom line is that you will not have a successful real estate business without lead generation. You must have a steady stream of interested prospects talking to you or someone in your business.

And the interesting thing about this is that, they will tell you that it's easy. We know this to be incorrect as well.

If it was easy, everyone would be doing it. Now, while it might not be easy, it is not overly complicated either. In this book, I will simplify this so you have a much better understanding and much clearer and realistic expectations.

See next page.

CHAPTER 3

Lead Generation Is Only 1 Part of Your Business

THIS IS IMPORTANT for you to know because most people get involved in the real estate industry with no intent or understanding that they'll be running a business.

Don't think about yourself as just an agent or just an investor. Think about yourself as running a real estate business. Being an agent or investor is just one part of your real estate business. You have many skills, and talents some that you bring from your careers and background before.

I have a client I was working with. He gave me a story about how one of his leads tracked him down to do business with him. This person wanted to do business with my client so bad that he messaged him on every platform he could. Facebook, Instagram, Text, DMs, etc.

"I'm so busy, I couldn't get back to this guy but first he messaged me on Facebook. Then he messaged me on Instagram, I couldn't respond. Then he emailed me. I finally got back to him and he signed up right away."

This was a client looking to pay $2500 for a real estate educational seminar. Luckily, this client was persistent. However, many other clients are not going to be this persistent about doing business with you. It is important that you follow up with your clients, customers, and prospects. Don't let your leads go to waste by not following up.

So here's how you should look at marketing and lead generation so you can run your real estate business successfully and never have to worry when you will close your next deal:

Lead Generation–This is the process of which you will generate hundreds or even, thousands of prospects that show interest in your services. There are usually lots of leads that come in this way and a majority of them will not convert.

Lead Follow-Up–This is a process of following up with the leads you have generated. Many businesses drop the ball here. They spend their hard-earned money and time working on getting these leads in but minimally follow up with them. This part can be difficult if you don't use the right system for this. Fortunately, with online media and marketing, you can use *"remarketing"* and *"retargeting"* to easily follow up with interested prospects. Simply put, remarketing and retargeting is when you follow up with a lead/prospect that has shown interest in your services or business.

Lead Conversion–This is where you have nurtured your leads. They are familiar with you, your business, or your services. This is where you will focus on actually getting them to do business with you. It's cliche... but remember, people do business with people they *know, like,* and *trust.*

Referrals–Here's another place where many drop the ball. By simply asking your client if they know anyone else that needs real estate services, you can increase your business. You've done all the work here and you've gotten them to the finish line. Don't let your efforts go to waste. Ask the simple question, "Do you know of anyone else that needs help in real estate?" and you might be surprised who people will refer to you. Normally, the best time to ask is right after the transaction, because you are still top of mind and your clients have just had a great experience.

CHAPTER 4

Math Matters & Success Is In The Percentages

THIS IS IMPORTANT for you to know because many are under the impression that you need to have high percentages to achieve success in the industry. This is simply not the case.

I had just finished teaching several agents my *Marketing Math Presentation*. One particular attendee reached out to me and said, "Jerome, I don't know what to do. Everything is broken. I don't know where to start in my business."

I simply asked him, "How many leads are you working on?" He said 1. 1 lead. Knowing what I have learned in the industry, I instantly knew this was not a great position for this student to be in. Working on 1 lead? The real estate industry is a business that is easier to understand once you do some basic math.

So here's what you need to do so you can set realistic expectations around lead generations and marketing in your real estate business:

Why Numbers Matter–The average conversion rate within the real estate industry ranges from 3%–5%. Furthermore, The National

Association of Realtors has published stats stating that the average conversion rate is 0.4% -1.2%. Think about it. 1% of 1 lead is less than 1. This means we have a very minimal chance of generating consistent business using these numbers. How can we improve this? By adding more leads.

Let's add some zeros so this can start to make more sense...

1% of 100 = 1 deal; 2% of 100 =2 deals; 3% of 100 = 3 deals.

3% of 100 = 3 deals; 3% of 200 =6 deals; 3% of 300 = 9 deals.

See how the numbers give clarity? Oftentimes, agents/investors are simply not working on enough leads in their business. Of course, these numbers will vary and fluctuate, depending on your market, relationships, etc. but at minimum, we want to have a system that is constantly working on increasing our lead flow. So we are not just working on 1 lead. The more leads we're able to generate and follow up on, the more success you will achieve and the more money you will make.

CHAPTER 5

The Fortune Is In
The Followup

THIS IS IMPORTANT for you to know because it will set you apart from other real estate agents and investors.

Again, many of us spend a great deal of time generating leads but what separates the successful from the unsuccessful is consistent follow-up. All you have to do is check Google and you'll find a ton of stats that prove this theory.

Here are some stats that you will find to be important to you:

44% of salespeople give up after one follow-up attempt (Scripted.com).

92% of salespeople give up after no sales on the 4th call (nugrowth.com).

60% of customers say no four times before saying yes (nugrowth.com).

Those who attempted to reach leads within one hour are 7x times more likely to have meaningful conversations with decision-makers than those who waited even 60 minutes (Harvard Business Review).

So here's what you need to do so you can follow up with your leads consistently and close more deals:

Set proper expectations for your business–understand that most leads will not convert or be ready to do business the first few tries. You will need to build a relationship with them first.

Remarket and retarget–follow-up does not have to be complicated. You can employ simple but effective remarketing and retargeting strategies using social media and other digital marketing strategies.

Use custom audiences, video marketing–use video marketing with your strategy this way you can create effective custom audiences and work with those who are actually interested and what it is that you are offering. Here is a quick example, if you create a video that is 3 minutes long, you can then create an audience of people who have finished that 3-minute video. This way you can effectively follow up with those that have shown a specific interest in your services.

CHAPTER 6

Social Media Yields Fast and Efficient Results

THIS IS IMPORTANT for you to know because there is a lot of confusion around social media marketing and it's hard to understand what is right and what is wrong.

One time, I received a message from a real estate agent out of anger and frustration. The tone of the letter was angry for sure. You may see me present and speak about this letter of frustration from time-to-time. I won't discuss the entire letter here. However, toward the end of the letter, this frustrated real estate agent asked me a very interesting question regarding all the marketing methods and marketing strategies: "Who is right?"

The interesting thing is that they're all pretty much right. Just about all strategies work when done *correctly* and *consistently*. However, many people go directly to social media because it's one of the more familiar ways to get your message out to your sphere of influence (SOI).

So here's what you need to do so you can pick up some business using Social Media and Social Media Marketing:

Social media is cost-effective–using social media and digital marketing strategies you can get immediate results instead of going out to pay expensive companies. You can pay money directly to social media. A lot of times when others are buying leads from Zillow, Realtor.com, and other similar sites, the sites are getting those leads from social media and other online sources that you have access to already. Using social media helps you go right to the source, effectively cutting out the middleman and saving you money on your lead generation and marketing.

Social media shouldn't be your only strategy–although social media can be effective and efficient, it should not be your only lead generation strategy. Social media marketing should be a complement to the other strategies in your business.

Facebook/Meta is usually the fastest/easiest to learn–Facebook is normally the easiest of each platform to learn. Facebook/Meta also owns Instagram so it is only a matter of a checkbox for you to advertise and market your business on the Instagram platform.

So now you know what you need to know about generating real estate leads so you know when and where your next real estate deal will be coming from and this is a good start.

But now you're probably asking:

CHAPTER 7

So What Do I Do Next?

If you're looking for the *fastest and easiest* way to get the results you desire, I've put together a very special no-cost, no-obligation, very limited-time offer just for you.

"60-Minute Lead Generation Frustration Elimination Consultation"

I have set aside space in my calendar to personally meet with you and lay out a customized plan to help you get the *Consistent Real Estate Leads Converted Into Cash* you want.

During our time together you will receive/discover:

60-Minute Lead Generation Frustration Elimination Strategy Session -

so you can walk away with a clear picture of all your options for creating a lead generation plan. (**$397 Value**)

My Content Creation Frustration Elimination Workshop Recording/Seminar -

so you know how to never run out of relevant content to talk about as a real estate professional. **($197 Value)**

Facebook Ads For Real Estate Checklist -

so you know what you need to set up your Facebook Lead Generation correctly. **($97 Value)**

I'm so confident that you'll find the *"60-Minute Lead Generation Frustration Elimination Strategy Session"* valuable that I'm going to give you my…

My 100% Risk-FREE Guarantee

Although your Strategy Session is free, I know your time is valuable. I also understand you might be wondering if my offer is as valuable as I say it is.

So I'm putting my money where my mouth is.

If after our time together, you don't feel it was worth your time, just tell me and I will *give you a 6-month FREE membership* **($497 Value)** *to our REmarketing Membership Portal so you can have access to top lead generation and marketing strategies that you can use to generate leads fast. …And you can keep any bonus material.*

Imagine if you could wave a magic wand and actually see *Consistent Real Estate Leads Converted Into Cash* taking place in your life.

I can help you make that happen.

The first step is to call or text my office at 267-888-1085 and say "I want to take advantage of *Jerome's Lead Generation Frustration Elimination Strategy Session.*" And we will get you all set up.

Sincerely,

Jerome Lewis

Chief Marketing Officer

P.S. If you don't feel comfortable taking that step, your next best option would be to read my #1 Best-Selling Book, REmarketing–Real Estate Marketing: Insider's Secrets of Successful Advertising, Lead Generation, & Marketing Implementation For Real Estate Entrepreneurs:

P.P.S. I understand if you're a bit skeptical. Many of my happy clients felt the same way before they met with me but here is what they found:

Other Resources

1. Register Your Book

To receive the FREE companion guide and Digital Real Estate Strategy Toolkit which contains valuable downloads, guides, and worksheets that will help you employ marketing implementation into your business... visit the website below.

2. Check Out Our Membership Portal

If you want access to our entire educational platform, including access to real estate investing resources, events, workshops, education, and more, become a REmarketing Member by visiting the below website.

3. Tune In To The REmarketing Podcast

If you're looking to stay ahead of the curve in the worlds of marketing, tech, and business, then the REmarketing Podcast is for you. Each week, we'll bring you insights and interviews from some of the brightest minds in these industries. So whether you're just starting out or are a seasoned pro, there's something for everyone here. Tune in now!

4. Marketing Implementation Course

Are you looking for a course that will teach you how to use social media and marketing to grow your business?

Look no further than Digitize! This comprehensive course will provide you with all the tools and knowledge you need to implement effective social media and marketing strategies.

You will learn how to create and execute campaigns that drive results, engage with your audience, and grow your brand.

In addition, you will get access to exclusive resources and templates that will save you time and help you achieve success.

Enroll today and start growing your business with social media and marketing!

Visit:

5. *Goal & Business Planner For Real Estate Entrepreneurs*

ATTENTION! Serious Real Estate Entrepreneurs Only: This Planner Is Guaranteed To Bring Clarity To Your Business & Business Goals!

Achieve Your Goals With Laser Focus

Stay Accountable To Yourself And Achieve More

Transform Your Business And Life For The Better

Set You Up For Success In Every Area Of Your Life

Get A Structured And Proven System For Goal Setting

Transform Your Business So You Can Achieve The Success You Never Thought Possible

>>> REmarketingBook.com/Planner <<<

May I Ask a Personal Favor?

If you have found value in this book or any of my work, please leave an honest review at an online bookstore. Whichever site you purchased the book from, please leave your review there. If you were gifted the book, please add your review to any major online book store, such as Amazon. I greatly appreciate honest feedback and reviews. It allows me to continue serving people like you.

If you are reading a physical copy, you can scan the QR code below.

Sincerely,

Jerome Lewis
Chief Marketing Officer

About The Author

JEROME LEWIS, HOST of the REmarketing Podcast, is a #1 Best-Selling Author that has authored 7+ books, including The Ultimate Video Marketing Guidebook For Real Estate Entrepreneurs & The #1 Best Selling REmarketing–Real Estate Marketing: Insider's Secrets of Successful Advertising, Lead Generation, & Marketing Implementation For Real Estate Entrepreneurs.

He is also the founder and CMO of Digital Real Estate Strategy, a tech, and marketing agency that helps busy but serious real estate entrepreneurs implement, structure, and systematize their tech, lead generation, marketing, and business systems. Jerome has helped over 5000 real estate entrepreneurs from more than 40 states and 4 countries. Jerome has shared stages with and worked with some of the real estate industry's best national experts including names ranging from Vena Jones-Cox, Krista Mashore, Marc Halpern, the Legendary Ron LeGrand, and many more.

Jerome is a bold introvert, father, and former IT professional. In 2021, Jerome won eXp Realty University's Instructor of The Year Award for his outstanding contribution to helping real estate agents grow their businesses through his proven tech and marketing strategies. He is also the host of the Real Estate Marketing Implementation & Social Media Mastermind Group, where he teaches real estate investors and agents tech and marketing implementation.

Work With Us

Visit https://UltimateMarketingAsset.com/Free-Gift.

We have done with you and done for you education and services to help you achieve success with your ultimate marketing asset. We hope to see you soon!